Save on Professional Fees, Plan Events Yourself

A Quick-How to on Planning Like a Pro

By: Linda Smith

9781635015003

I0510829

PUBLISHERS NOTES

Disclaimer – Speedy Publishing LLC

Speedy Publishing LLC

40 E Main Street, Newark, Delaware, 19711

Contact Us: 1-888-248-4521

Website: http://www.speedypublishing.co

REPRINTED Paperback Edition: 9781635015003:

Manufactured in the United States of America

DEDICATION

This book is dedicated to Manuel. The moment I saw you, I knew that I was going to marry you. Thank you for making every second of our married life a dream I don't want to wake up from. I love you to the moon and back.

TABLE OF CONTENTS

CHAPTER 1- FACTORS THAT DEFINE A SUCCESSFUL EVENT

There are many factors that make an event successful, however, there are just nine listed here that will make your event a definite success. You will have to pay attention to all details of the event and make sure that you stay on top of things for the event to really take off.

First, you need to make sure that you plan everything. You should plan for the best, worst, and expected scenes. When you do this you end up having all your bases covered. You have backup plans to help you with your problems and you also don't have time to panic because you've planned that well. You need to make sure that you look at everything. What's the worst that can happen?

Save on Professional Fees, Plan Events Yourself
Always plan for the worst because you will never know what will happen in the future.

While you are planning, make sure that you stay organized. The worst thing that you can do is throw all your beautiful plans in one big pile and expect to find things at last minute or lose vital information. To stay organized you need to keep all your contracts and important information in a binder. When you keep things in the bind you know exactly where everything is and what you need to do at all time. However, bind the papers. When you bind the papers you are more likely to not lose all the information in some accident. Also, make sure you have it on you at all times so that you can immediately put things in the binder.

To start the party off on the right foot, you need to make sure that you pick the right venue, theme, and everything else. When it comes to the right venue, you need to make sure that all your guests can come to the place without ease and that it is appropriate for the event. You don't want to have a ball at a hunting lodge, or maybe you do, it just depends on what you want the night to say. Right from the start you can have a perfect event by selecting the perfect place to hold the event.

Once you have picked out your location you can then begin to plan the event. The first thing that you need to plan when it comes to the event is the theme. Make sure that your theme is exactly what you are going for. You need to use your theme to help coordinate all the other details of the event and the theme will help you in making some very important decisions. In fact, the theme is everything. It is the first thing that you should define.

Once you have the theme you can then think about the party or event. There are two important factors of every event, they just so happen to be the food and drinks. You will want to make sure that you form a contract with some of the best caters in the area to ensure that your party or event ends splendidly. Also, you should know that this is so important that it can literally make or break your event. With bad food comes bad ratings and you're sure thing for failure. Once you have booked the caterers and sampled everything you will feel more confident. Also, think about the drinks. You may not want to offer a cash bar or open bar. They both can be expensive in their own ways, however, if you limit your bar you can make it seem like an open bar, but you can limit your budget.

Once you have the food and drinks planned you can move onto entertainment. You will want something that will keep your guests entertained and be educational and fun. You can have a band or singer to help entertain. If you are a charity, you should make sure that you inform your audience about the cause and the importance of their help, most of all, donations.

To help you with everything you need to have good venders. Venders are what make the party. You should always be kind to your suppliers because you never know when you will need them the most. Don't be surprised if mistreated vendors breech contract and not even show up. You'll look ridiculous not having a dinner minutes before the dinner.

Finally, you should think about how you can do all of this and still keep your cool. You may want to hire an assistant or have someone help you with all the to-do lists. However, you may find that you don't trust anyone to be responsibly enough, but you should at least give people a try.

Planning an event can be hard for anyone. You will find that the task is just too big for just one person; this is why most people will have a team or assistants to help them with all the little details. There are a lot of things that you need to look out for when planning your event, but if you take the time to dedicate to planning the party or event, you should be fine.

The first thing that you need to avoid when planning an event is not to get overwhelmed. You don't want to get overwhelmed because it will only make things worse. Not only will you have a bad party, but you will also be fluttered and frustrated into doing things that you shouldn't. You need to gain control over the event instead of letting the event gain control over you. You need to make sure that that everything is okay one piece at a time. For instance, one day you should take care of the decorations and the next day deal with the venders. This way you aren't taking on too much at once. You may also hire an assistant to help you or you may find that things can get too much. If you are having a very important event, you should always have a team to help you so that you can find ways to quickly solve those last minute blunders.

You should also take a lot of time to pick the menu. The menu is one of the biggest reasons why people love or hate an event. Make sure that you have just exactly what you need to make the guests happy. You may want to try new things so that the party is a little bit spicy and you don't want to be compared to some other party or event. You can make your mark with the food. If the food is good, the party will go off without a hitch. However, just because you pick out great foot doesn't mean that things will work out. You also need to make sure that you use vendors that are responsible and have a reputation of being the best. This is so you know that they will deliver the food and without any problems. If the food is bad or missing, your guests will spread all those nasty rumors about your party.

You need to also think about your contracts. You should have a contract written up with all your vendors. You will be much happier knowing that you have a formal business contract. The contract is your safety net. You can take the vendor to court if there is a breach of contract, however, you should know the contract works both ways. You can find yourself in some trouble if you back out on a contract. Contracts are very important when it comes to any event or business transaction. They work for you when the vendor falls through.

Not only should you always have a contract, but you should also always make sure that you don't go bankrupt over an event. You need to watch out for that budget. If you tend to splurge you should lower your budget. This way when you go over you have hit the real budget. This is just one of the ways that you can psych yourself out and stick with the budget. Also, you should know that you need to make sure that you count every expense. When the party is said and done, you don't want to deal with any unexpected or forgotten bills.

CHAPTER 2- HOW TO ADD FUN TO ANY EVENT

When it comes to entertainment, you should try to provide it without having to spend a lot of money. You can find many ways to incorporate entertainment into the event without spending a bomb by following some of the following tips. These tips should be helpful to either help generate your own money saving ideas or they might be the solution that you seek.

The first option that you have is to ask some of the local celebrities to help host or show up at the event. When you do this, you can ask them to donate their time or even a few minutes to the event. It will help the charity sell tickets and you can find some good entertainment without having to pay a thing. If that doesn't help, you may want to still take advantage of your local community.

Linda Smith

When it comes to the bank or singer, you should look in your local community. You will be surprised at what kind of entertainment that you can find and you will also thank yourself for finding a band or singer with a low rate. Most of the time, the local bands will work events in order to get their name out there and for exposure. You may need to give them a free dinner, but it beats having to spend thousands of dollars on entertainment. You will find plenty of ways to cut the entertainment costs, but nothing like hiring some locals.

If you really do want to get a celebrity you can go about it in two ways. First, you can always have a celebrity come to the event purely to donate a few minutes. This will be a free service for them, but also a tax deduction. Just because they aren't donating their money, they are donating something of significance. You should also think about raising money to hire someone.

If you get a committee together and have everyone donate some money in order to have entertainment, you will be able to get practically any star to show up. If celebrities aren't your thing, then you can always just the money you put together to hire some local unknowns or to help out with the event planning in general.

When it comes to hiring a band or a DJ, you need to think about a few things. Not only have you had to pay one guy, but all the band mates. When you hire a DJ you only have to pay for one or two people to set time aside for you. You should also know that DJs usually come with their own permits, if you have a band you may need to find someone to get you a permit for the performance. Usually, a DJ only takes a little bit of your space up too; a band can take a whole room up depending on its size.

However, if you have your heart set on a performer, you should think about paying for them to play for an hour or two. This way you don't have to pay for the night, but just for a few hours. This will cut your entertainment costs in half. This is a good thing to keep in mind when your budget seems to be getting smaller and smaller. When you rent a band for an hour or two, you can keep things going great and not have to worry about the costs.

If you really want to make things memorable, you might want to think about things like hiring a comedian or some other person to perform an act other than music. This way you can put some humor into the event and everyone will laugh the night away. It will also make things seem more comfortable when it comes to serious matters. A joke can go a long ways, but it may not with every budget.

You may just want to sit down and think about what your resources are and if you have any connections. You may find that someone knows someone who can do you a favor. You never know what you will find when you pull the committee together.

The Secrets to a Memorable Gathering

When it comes to an event, you need to make sure that you make it educational, entertaining, and memorable. This is extremely important when you have to place a charity event in the making. So what makes an event all these things? Well you should look at each of them separately. What can you do to make an even educational? What can you do to make it entertaining? What will make this a memorable event that no one will be able to forget?

First, look at the educational aspect. What is the charity or event for? You need to state your purpose or goal everywhere. You can do this in several ways. Once way that you can be educational is by placing stands or show pieces around the event like an art show. Place random facts on the walls or on display so that you can get your guests thinking. You can put on a movie or documentary about the charity and show the people first-hand what is really going on and why they should help. You could also do a speech with the help of visual aids to help support your charity. All of these are great ideas when it comes to making something educational, but what about entertaining.

Well if you want just entertainment you can have a band or singer perform at the event. However, that can be expensive. If you are having a charity, you should make sure that you mix entertainment with educational. Basically, you should try to find ways like through plays and other art forms to entertain and to educate. You never know how creative you can get until you try to mix education and entertainment. When you try to mix them you will find that your creativity will pour out ideas and you'll have success in doing so. You need to make sure that the entertainment is clean and fun, especially for charity events.

While you are thinking about how to make things entertaining and educational, you may just want to add some remarkable details in the mix. When you add some things like fireworks or celebrities in the mix, your guests are going to remember the event for most of their lives. You don't have to invite any celebrities to make a memorable event. You can do things by picking a unique venue or by having some of the most special and unique details in the event. There are hundreds of things you can do to make a party remarkable. You should do some activities to get the creativity flowing so that you are able to make an impression on all your guests. You will want to make sure that you add something special into the mix so that everyone will be more willing to donate large sums of money or at least some money.

When you have try to include information, entertainment, and shocking or fun events, you are more than likely to reach your goal and surpass any expectations that you may have. You will find that you will be happy with the results from the event. The only hard part about it is finding the creative ideas. If you take some time in your planning, you should have no trouble coming up with ideas and having a wonderful event. You will want to make sure that you have done everything to make things go as smoothly as possible. That includes staying organized so that you are able to find all the information upon needing and also you can stay on top of things. You will have a great event when you take the time to really care about the event and see things through.

Tips on Making Your Event Exciting and Interesting

There are plenty of ways that you can make an event interesting and exciting. You will need to let your creativity flow and not hinder you. The way that you do this is simply by brainstorming. Every time that you come up with an idea you should write it down. At this point you don't want to judge the idea. Some of the worst ideas can turn into being a blessing. Even if your ideas seem silly and outrageous you should still write it down. At the brainstorming stage you don't judge your ideas. This process will help you come up with hundreds of ideas and then later narrowed to a few good ideas.

The first tip to coming up with making your even interesting and exciting has to deal with the point of the event. If you can, you should have famous entertainers to help out with the cause. This way you can bring people in with your celebrities, but then you are able to save some money on the interesting aspects of the event. You should always make sure that they are willing to donate their time so that you don't end up paying, making this tip one of the most interesting concepts of the event. You should also think about what kind of person you would like to help with the event, rather it be a singer, actor, or dancer.

You should also think about the food. When it comes to the food you can do a lot for an event. You can make it exciting and interesting easily by adding some exotic foods. You may also want to blend your ability to offer some foods that are traditional for an event of this kind and some food that is wild and new.

When it comes to planning an event ahead of time, you will find that your ideas will be pouring in, however, it comes a time when you hit a wall. You don't know what to do or how to present an aspect of the event. This is when you have to do some things to generate the ideas

Another way you may be able to generate some interest is not just by having high celebrities, but some of the local celebrities as well. This way you can get the community to back your guest and to open them to the event with open arms. You will find that most of the local TV personalities are more than willing to offer some help in the name of charity. However, if you aren't a charity you may want to think about other things that don't cost a lot of money and you don't have to fuss over. Once of these things would be some interesting facts.

If you do a lot of research, you are able to entertain your audience with facts. You can celebrate your numbers and you will find it to be a rush. However, you should make sure that the facts are true. The last thing that you need is to read in the newspaper tomorrow about how you lied. You don't have to stretch the truth to have interesting facts.

If education isn't the thing then entertainment is. If you would like to have some examples of entertainment you can go with dancers, singers, and actors. This way you can entertain your guests and be able to celebrate how well your wallet is doing. Basically if you are able to find some local school to help you out with the entertainment, you can cut your costs in half.

Do something outrageous as well. Hire someone to set off fireworks or have sky divers. This will make your party unique and special. To have an entertaining party you may also want to think about the drinks. You may want to expand the bar or to decrease. Alcohol is a great way to start a party, but it's no way to celebrate for one.

You may also want to go online and help with you entertainment. You never know who you might be able to book to make the party out of this site. If you have your people call their people, this will work out great.

Another way to add some excitement is by adding some animals to the batch. The animals will make the party wild and crazy. Everyone will love this outrageous party.

You may also want to add some excitement with the music. Make the music go with the theme of the party and go wild on the dance floor.

Finally, you may want to have several things going on at once. This way you can have everyone entertained to keep things interesting and entertaining.

Chapter 3- The Beautiful Truth and Benefits of Teambuilding in Events

For any event, you will need to think about teambuilding elements so that you can have a strong front and make the plans turn into good actions. When you find out how to work within a team you are able to not only function together, but solve things much quicker than by yourself. With a successful team you are able to get things done fast, on time, and right. You have more resources as a team than trying to do everything yourself. You need to be able to have a team that can be make neutral decisions by themselves and as a group. You need to use teambuilding elements in your event planning just so that you can get the event into motion and not have to worry about doing it all yourself.

When you are first bringing a team together you need to find out who is compatible with your work ethics and who isn't. You will find that some people will naturally but-heads, but you will also find that some people just make a great team. You should allow them to experiment to see who wants to be partnered with whom else. You can do this by letting nature take its course. You will find that they will naturally flock to one person more than others. This is a good sign to let you know who should be partnered. You need to do some team building activities to make sure that everyone is able to come together and work together for a common goal. These activities can be anything that you wish. You will find that any task will prove who can work with whom; however, you should encourage others to work with everyone so that you have an all about successful team.

When you build teamwork, you need to watch out for some things. You shouldn't always let one couple work with each other. This will bring separation in the group and the goal is to find unity. You should also watch for those who distract each other. You want to find partners that will focus on the main goal and then take steps to that goal. You will want to make sure that you keep the partners changing so that everyone gets a chance to work with everyone. This will help unity form, as well as, a strong partnership bond.

Once you have a strong partnership, you will find that the group will be able to be more independent, and they will find ways to quickly solve any issues that come up. You should know that it will make the work go faster and with better quality. When you have a group of people looking out for the common good, you will have an improvement in quality.

When it comes to having a team, you need to have a leader to have some control over the situation. You will be the leader in whom all the groups will confide in when making major decisions and asking for opinions. You should try to keep things going in the group when they hit a stalemate. You need to only help your teams out when the productivity levels have gone drastically for the worst. You will keep the groups on track so that they can always be reaching for the common goal.

When you use teams to help you with your event, you will find that everything goes smooth and that you fix issues quicker than ever. With the help from a team, you should be able to find a path, stay on the path, and have some fun while working towards a common goal.

How to Incorporate Effective Team Building

When it comes to team work you will need it for most of your events. You will need to think about the teamwork first. You will have plenty of little details that must be completed, but can you put the most effect team together? When it comes to choosing people to be on a team, you have to pick them for a reason other than personal. You need to know that they are able to make decisions and get things done. They have to be goal oriented, however, you should also think about the way that they can come together and find easy and quick solutions to any of the problems that may pop up.

First, when bringing a team together, you need to get them to bond. The way to get a team to bond is to give them a simple task and then watch how they work with each other. Some people will bump heads quickly and then some will come together and really focus on the task at hand. You should make sure that you pair the team so that they will work to your advantage. You should make sure that each person has something to bring to the table. When it comes to activities that will build team spirit, you may want to think about letting the group divide itself. Partners tend to work better when they are placed with others whom they wish to be with. This however, can also be the devil in disguise. Not only can this work to your advantage, but you may eventually have to separate them because they distract each other from the task at hand.

However, to build team bonding you need to make sure that you allow the teams to have most or complete control over things. You will find that if you add some competition in with the mix which of the groups will perform better. You can do this by setting the group into two smaller groups with the same task and then see which team can pull it through. Then you can get some feedback and see if you have someone ruining your perfect team equation. When you find out that there is someone ruining your team, you can either pull them from the project or give them smaller and insignificant tasks to seem like they are helping.

If you need a team to improve on their teambuilding skills, you will need to set them aside and tell them out you feel. You can let out that you are disappointed. This way you can motivate them to put things in gear, but you may need to talk to the group members about why they are falling behind and try to find a solution. Sometimes you will find that your teams will be ineffective because of one person and that may be the time to let someone go. However, if it is crunch time you need to get everyone working together successfully.

For the process of planning the event, you need to delegate activities or roles within the groups and then keep an open door. Hence, you are able to find out what and where the trouble is coming from, and how to take the right measures. When you are trying to keep a team going you have to act as manager and sometimes you need to be touch and sometimes sympathetic.

As for the activities that you do to help build good team work, you can get creative with them, but make sure that your tests or tasks

Linda Smith

is a part of the bigger plan. This way you can get things done and the others can learn about the importance of teamwork.

CHAPTER 4- NUMBERS COUNT IN EVENT MANAGEMENT

When it comes to planning a small event and a big event, you will notice a huge change. You should be aware that it will make the entire planning process change. When you have a small event, you can plan with a breeze, but when it comes to planning for larger events, you should know that it comes at a very different price.

The most important thing about planning a smaller event then a bigger event is that you don't have as much as a hassle with details. Small events are often casually planned because they are usually your friends and they sympathize with you. However, when you have guests that hardly know you, it's a big deal about everything. You should know that there is quite a list of things that you need to do to have a fabulous party event, however, when you are only caring for ten people; you tend to overlook the smaller details. When it comes to managing a smaller event you are able to make quick decisions, but when you have to throw a party for 100, your options are limited.

That's the next point; with bigger parties your options are limited. You can't just decide one day that you would like to have duck and then the next have ham. If you are getting it catered, the supplier will tell you that your requests can not be dealt with in such a small time; however, they can easier find the foods that you wish to have for a small group of ten. Also, with the food comes the drinks and that can be quite an expense. You should know that an open bar can be expensive even for ten, but it can be even more costly when it comes to asking for a cash bar. So the solution to your problem for both cases is to limit your drinks. With a small party you can have two or three different kinds, but with a larger party, you may have to offer more. Depending on your guests, the event, and the budget, the drinks could be less than expected for any type of party.

Once you have gotten over the food and drinks, you then have to think about the seating. Not only do you have to plan to sit ten people, but ten times that. However, when it comes to seating, the larger events have the upper hand. You are able to be able to place your guests with either people they like or don't know, but can easily avoid those who despise each other. This can be a blessing if the event happens to be something like your wedding.

The budget is tightly affected by the size of the event. The smaller the event the smaller the budget can be, but you can spend and pay close attention to details with a smaller event. You will find that a small event can be one hell of a party, but with the larger parities, you tend to skip out on great ideas simply because they didn't fit into the budget. When it comes to budget, the smaller parties are in the lead, but there are so many discounts that you can get in bulk that the two options are almost tied.

There are so many more factors of planning an event that is affected by the size of the event. Usually smaller has a lot of benefits to the guests and the planner, but there are times that you just need to have a grand celebration and you need to be prepared to sink in the time to plan the event as well.

Logistics – Where the Real Work Begins

When it comes to event planning, there are some things that you will need to think about and take careful planning. You will need to make a lot of important decisions that will determine the outcome of your event. You should make sure that you pay attention to all your event details and make sure that you get exactly what you expected.

First, you need to understand the importance of a contract. Contracts are used in most if not all business transactions. If you hire a band, cater, venue, and other important critical factors, you need to get everything in writing. If you don't get everything in writing you will find out that you might be a big loser in the end. You need to get a contract when you agree to deal with any suppliers or venues. You need to protect yourself in case they don't live up to your expectations. The only thing is that everything needs to be written in the contract. With the contracts, you should have a good, solid back up plan.

When it comes to planning an event successfully, you will need to remain organized. If you are able to organize all your information into a binder you will always know where everything is. You can pull out anything that you need when you need it and not go searching through anything. It will make the plans go smoothly and you will be able to stay on top of things. Also, being organized has a lot of other benefits that will make the event look even better and very professional. It will also help you with your planning. Remember, you need to have a backup plan for everything. With an organized binder you can be one step ahead of things.

Linda Smith

You should also think about your suppliers and venues. You will want to keep professional relationships with them so that you are able to maintain the good relationships for other events and they will become loyal and go out of their way to help you with your events. When you play nice with the suppliers you will find it to be a huge pay off in the end and in the future. You will have good relations that will maintain stability in your plans. When you do something to upset a vender, you can basically expect them to not hold up their end of the deal. Contracts are nice legally, but at the time of the event, you have to rely on vender relationships. Contracts work afterwards in court.

You should also know that all your event details will play an active role. They will determine what kind of party that you have and how fun it will be for your guests. You should know that the venue is one of the most important things next to the food and drinks. The venue needs to be somewhere that everyone can get too easily. You need to at least get these people to come out, and then you can reel them in with the food, drinks, and entertainment. There are plenty of ways to reel your guests in, but the most successful one is by having a good and creative venue.

Then after you have decided on the venue you can then plan the rest of the party. You should place a huge emphasis on the food and drinks for the sake of the guests. When you take your time to think about the decisions of the food and drinks then you are more likely to please your guests, which is the main point of any event.

CHAPTER 5- WOW YOUR GUESTS UPON ARRIVAL AT YOUR VENUE

When it comes to transforming an event venue you can do a lot with nothing. You can change the whole mood of a place by following some of the easiest tips found here. You should be able to take a dark room and fill it with romance or make a silly room serious. All you have to do is think about the mood that you want and where you stand in progress. Usefully ever venue needs some decorations to make things seem easier to fit into the events ambiance.

First, you need to add a splash of color and boldness. You can add some boldness by getting some nice things like cloths and other decorations to bundle or design your room with. If you get a lot of long sheets of interesting fabric you will be able to add both color and boldness to the venue. You can let them hang from the ceiling or have them gently flow through the room. Your creativity has no limits when it comes to adding colors and boldness. The only thing that you want to avoid is colors that will be too bright for the occasion. If you are going for romance stick with red hues; if you are going for party, stick with some of the brighter and bold colors. The decorations are at your discretion, but first, you need to make sure that you don't have any limits because of venue rules. Simply ask before signing a contract with them.

You should also think about small, little things that will be great accents. You can go to make low-priced craft places and find a million things to use as accents. You may want to purchase a bag filled with seashells is you may want to use simple things like petals and pearls. When it comes to romance, you can't get any more romantic than with rose petals and pearl beads. If you are on a budget, you can find plenty of things like fake crystals, pieces of glass, stones, and other things to place on the tables to accent the place. If using smaller objects to give the venue a hint of mood changing, you can change the complete look by assign height.

When you go to ass some height you will want to use tall things to add some height to the room. You may want to use things like pillars or candle holders to get the dimension going. If you have a small place, the height will give you some added depth to the place. You should also know that if you use tall center pieces, this will work too. The only thing is that you want to make sure that the items will not easily be knocked over. This can save a lot of your guests from being hurt.

Also, if you use a matching décor, you can take out of the darkness and add a good bit of color. However, you don't want too much color so if you match the tablecloths with the floor runner or to some of the other decorations it will all seem to come together. If that doesn't do the trick, then flowers will.

When you use flowers you are able to change the room entirely. This tends to make everything seem brighter and glowing. If you want radiance, you should order some flowers to be set down here and there. You don't have to go overboard on the flowers, but if you watch your budget, you should be able to squeeze precious flowers in here and there.

However, maybe it is not the décor of the room, but the size of the room that bothers you. If you change the tables in the venue, you will be able to make the room feel smaller or bigger. For rooms or venues that are smaller, you should add round tables in the place. The round tables will give the illusion that there is more room, and also your guests will be able to feel it. If you would like to make a larger room appear to be smaller you can always add long tables into the mix.

The last tip is the lighting. The lighting is everything in a mood. If you want people to be aware and place bids or donations, you will want the lighting to be fairly bright. This will get the attention of the guests, but it won't give them a headache. You should also dim the lights if you want a night of romance and passion to be present.

How to Choose the Right Venue

You need to be careful when you are planning an event of any type. There are so much to do and so many different mistakes that you can make at the same time. You will find that it is easy to get lost and lose your sense of great ideas early in the event planning process. You want to try and make the most of the ideas that you have so that you can make this type of even the most successful and memorable for everyone.

You must make sure that your event is taking on the personality that you want. You do not want to shock anyone with a totally different venue that they are not going to love. Your biggest feat is to make sure that everyone is going to have a great time so that this can be the best party of the year. Doing this does not have to be hard. In fact, you can have the most talked about party of the year if you really set your mind to it.

You need to look out for certain things when it comes to choosing your event venue. You need to be sure that you are planning fun for everyone. You need to have the event jam packed with fun and excitement so that anyone that attends is going to have something great to do. They will be excited to be there and afterwards, they will be glad that they came.

Another thing to look out for when you are planning a great event is the food. You need to make sure that you are able to find a menu that everyone is going to love. You will want to meet the needs of all the different types of guests to ensure that they have the best dinner that they have ever had. If you are having children at your party, you will want to accommodate their needs as well. You will certainly want something great for them to munch on.

You should also make sure that the area that you have the event is going to be best for the occasion. You need to find somewhere that will fit all of your guests comfortably so that no one is uncomfortable and feeling like they are cramped together. The most room that you have will mean that the more people you can invite. Remember that you want to make sure that you are using a place that will keep your guests in one area and allow them to mingle, as they should be. You will see that your guests will have a better time if they are all meeting and chatting along in the same area. You do not want them to be scattered around or separated.

Getting what you want from your event is not going to be easy. You will have to make sacrifices and use a lot of your resources. You may also have to hire someone to help you along and get you through this difficult time. When you are able to find some help with your event, you will feel a lot better and you may also see that your event goes a lot smoother as well. This is something that you can be proud of and excited about at the same time. Planning a great event that has minimal flaws is not easy, but it something that you will be proud of at the same time.

Getting there to the perfect party is something that will be grueling and of course you are going to make mistakes, however you will learn from it and do better the next time you are planning the perfect party.

What Kind of Guests Should You Expect?

There are many different types of events and there are different people who you will like to attract to the party, however, you need to attract the right people to the event or it just won't be the same.

One of the best ways to attract the right people is make your party a private party. Private parties are invitation only. When you have a private party you are able to limit the amount of people who will attend and also the type of people that will come. This is when you can send it to all the people that you truly would like at the party. However, just because you invite them, doesn't mean that they will come. So how do you get the people who really want to come to the party?

Linda Smith

The way to get all those important people that you want to come to your party is offer them something they can't refuse. On the invitation, which should be professionally done, you will want to say something encouraging. Things like you are invited to the ____'s party of the year or a night of romance and dining. Most people will not turn down a dinner party because it is a way for them to associate and mingle with possible business associates.

To weed out the unwanted, you should state on the invitation the dress code. Like black tie event, or semi-formal/formal. Usually, the more emphasis on formal, the more likely you are able to weed out all those who wouldn't fit in. Most people will not attend a party if they feel uncomfortable. If you would like to invite someone who wouldn't fit in, go ahead, because at least you can say that you offered, but most likely they won't come and ruin the party by their antics.

Another way to get the people whom you really want to come is by giving them a VIP ticket to the party. This way they can come and associate with other people whom you think is very important to the party, but they don't have to deal with all the hassle of associating with those whom they would rather not. VIP also makes a person feel very special and honored. With the word VIP, they are more likely to come because it is an honor. It is one way to lure the best guests to come to a party or event.

You need to hire a publicist to help you plan a huge event for you. Your publicist will do everything for the party. They will advertise how great the party is and they will also show you ways to enhance your public look. They will make your look and act like a VIP without being a VIP. A publicist will help you look ten times better. They know exactly what it takes to get the ideal guests to attend and what you need to do to persuade them to come.

Save on Professional Fees, Plan Events Yourself

One of the best times to throw a party is when you are moving up the ladder. This way you can have people whom you have become friends with and also make some business contacts. Getting the important people to the party can be hard, but many of them are interested in the new person. They want to know the person who may, someday, replace them. That's one reason why you might get them to come, however, you need to consider that when it comes to the party. You need to think about why they are coming and then deliver all that they expect from the party, your family, and your home so that they keep you mind.

Chapter 6- What To Avoid When Planning Events

When it comes to planning an event, it can be rough. You not only have to worry about all the details that are major, but you have to deal with all the little things. You may find that there are some reoccurring problems that you have when you plan events. Each problem that you run into should teach you some kind of lesson for the next event.

The first thing that you should avoid when it comes to planning your next event is getting overwhelmed with details. If the event is getting bigger and bigger and you've seem to lost control over things, you need to get backup. It's hard to plan an event, especially if it is a very important event. You have to plan where you are going to have the event, the theme, the decorations, the food, the caterers, the supplies, and the budget. You need to make sure that you stay within a budget, but get everything done. This is when you need an assistant.

If you don't have an assistant you will have an emotional breakdown and it could ruin the event. Depending on your personality, the breakdown can be crucial. This is way you need an assistant. Don't get overwhelmed with things. When it comes to using an assistant you can leave them the minor things like fetching, fixing, decorating, and all the small details that you should never worry about.

The second pitfall that you need to avoid is the bar and food. If you are going to have a catered dinner or event, you need to make sure that you have a written contact upon hiring. The contract needs to state the money, the food, and basically what you expect from the amount of money that you are paying. Even put the time when they need to show up in the contract or you may end up with irresponsible caters. You need to make sure that the food looks and taste good. You don't want to have people looking at you with disappointment.

The third pitfall to avoid has to deal with contracts. Get a contract written for everything. It can be on a tablecloth, if you must. Just make sure that you have it in writing what you are paying them, why you are paying them, what you expect from them and the day and times that they need to show up with the goods. If you don't, you will end up having someone come to you saying that they overbooked or they have increased the costs.

The fourth pitfall to avoid is bankruptcy. Make sure that you set a budget for your event. The way to successfully set budget is to set a least and the most amounts. For example, you can pay at least $5,000 for the party, but you can go to $7,000. Then you aim for the average, so you would like to have a $6,000 party. If you set your budget like that you know exactly if you need to cut the corners or if you can expand somewhere on the party. You will also be more successful if you set yourself some limits. You'll be more likely to be under budget.

The fifth and final pitfall to avoid is relaxing too far in advance. A lot of people will plan an event so far ahead that they think that they can take it easy the day before or even the day of the party or event. You need to realize that when you find extra time to relax, make some phone calls. Make sure that everyone is on the same page so that when the day comes you don't run around like a chicken with its head cut off. You can take the day of the event with a relaxed pace because you were on top of things the day before.

Why Troubleshooting Skills Are a Must

Planning a big event is something that you will find to be trying at times. You will have a lot of things to do and you will find not enough time to do them in. you will feel rushed and maybe even a little bit anxious at the same time. You will not be able to make everything perfect and this is something that you will just have to deal with.

Anytime you are planning something, you will probably find that something goes wrong. You will not have an easy time with everything unless you are perfect and in real life that does not happen. You will want to make sure that you are prepared to take on the things that are going to happen so that you are able to deal with them and move on to the next item.

No matter how much planning you do for your special event, you will see that something will always be missed. This is usually the case even if you are double-checking and rechecking everything. You will want to make sure that you can handle mistakes and forgotten things that somehow go untaken care of when you are planning a special event.

You can get your party to run a little better when you are using a good checklist. This will be a list that will include all the things that you have to do for your party. Once they are accomplished, you can check them off and this will make your party planning a little easier and more organized as well. This is one thing that will be a great help to you and anyone that is helping you with the party as well.

If you are find that it is the day of the party and moments before the party is set to begin you see that something was missed, you can try your best to fix the situation. You may have to use a little bit of your creative side to come up with a quick fix, but you may surprise yourself with a great idea. You can be surprised at the way that your mind will think when you are in a bind and looking for an easy fix.

If you are at the event and noticing that something is not going right, you will want to try and fix the problem as fast as you can without anyone knowing about it. You may not want to draw a lot of attention to the problem that you are trying to fix. However you may want to find someone to help you with the situation and get a strong fix for it. This is something that you can do with the right amount of help. You can also have some of your friends going around the party and looking for things that need are going wrong. You may find that this is a huge help with things because you cannot be everywhere at one time.

The biggest thing that you need to do when you see that something is going off course at your event is to not get upset. You want to be able to stay calm and use your resources that you have to fix the problem. You should not panic and get all worked up because one thing is going wrong. You will find that once you get a hold of yourself and let your brain think, you will find a solution to anything that comes up. Who knows, you may not even have to worry about some of the small stuff that goes wrong. As long as you and everyone are having fun, you will have a very successful party.

Chapter 7- Planning Meetings and Corporate Events

When it comes to meetings, you have to come fully prepared and ready to state your side and then show all the documentation that you have used and collected. There are basically seven ways for you to have an easy and hassle free meeting plan.

The first thing that you must do is identify everything that you will need. Make sure that if you need an overhead projector that it is set up in the room before the meeting starts. You may want to come to the meeting an hour or two head and set the room. You need to make sure that all the equipment that you use is good and works. This is the time for you to set up the rest of the room. You may need to rearrange the furniture and other things to make sure that everyone can comfortably see the presentation. You may also want to take this time to set your table up. If you have folders or handouts that you would like to share with your associates, you may want to leave them at the end of the table or around the table.

Before you go to set up the meeting room, you should have an agenda. If it is your meeting and you are in charge, make sure that you have an agenda so that everyone knows exactly what the meeting is about. You can send them in emails or by fax so that everyone knows exactly what to come prepared for. This will make your meeting go smoothly because all the facts and documents that the group will need will be present. Since everyone will be aware of what the discussion is about they will come prepared with all their notes and facts.

If you are conducting the meeting, you will need a speech. You don't have to write a complete speech, but take note cards to remind you of the key points. This way you don't overlook a vital piece of your presentation. You can keep your note cards in your hands during the meeting, or you can leave them on the podium for reference.

If you aren't sure how long the meeting is going to be, you may want to cancel all your other meetings and dates for the rest of the day. This way you don't feel like you have to rush the presentation or meeting. Also, the other people whom you had set a schedule with will also appreciate the gesture.

When you go to set up the meeting, you should go through a practice run. This way you can calm your nerves and deliver a great speech. Also, you will know exactly what your speech will take time wise, so you can have a guess to how long the meeting will be. Then you can call your secretary and cancel any meetings that you may need to

Finally, the last tip that you should follow when it comes to giving a hassle free meeting is to talk to your secretary and ask them to hold any unimportant calls. However, you should talk to them what an emergency is. Unless it pertains to your family, then you should never accept any calls during the meeting. If you do decide to take a call, then you should leave the room and ask someone else to take over for a minute or ask the group to think about your presentation so far and you'll come back to clear any misunderstands once you've taken the call.

All these tips should help you have a smooth meeting and come to the meeting well prepared. When you go to a meeting prepared, the meeting will go as good as possible for you and your team or company.

Meetings Online: Can They Be Planned and Organized Like Everything Else?

Online Expos and parties are designed to put you in front of real live people in a chat system, and give you the opportunity to make new connections and gather leads, showcase your business, product or services and yes make some sales. It is first and foremost a great place to connect with others and get the word out about your business.

Online event and parties can put you in front of people but what you do with those opportunities, leads and contacts are up to you. Online events are all about vital and cooperative marketing. It is up to everyone involved to promote, tell your friends, tell your family and spread the word.

Linda Smith
What Is Cooperative Marketing?

What we are seeing is more and more people coming online and finding it a creative outlet for their business. Many however (like me in 1999) know very little about the World Wide Web aka internet aka Information Super Highway. It is a great and excellent tool but that is all it is. You can learn anything you may want about business, or pretty much everything else. You need others to help you online to be successful. People, because of the schemes and scams out there rarely do business with people they know right off the bat. And one person or one website is but a drop in the Internet Ocean, unless there is experience with advertising or knowledge of marketing but yet many seem to think a website is all your need. It is not that easy! If it were we would all be Thin and Rich. The internet will not create business for you; we still have to do that. But it can make things easier.

One of the trends we see that is growing are online events like this one, at my Network the Small Business Referral Network we started hosting online events over a year ago. And I was personally introduced to them in 2000 – 2001. Today there are more sites than you can shake a stick at and not all are created equal. Find a Group you feel good about joining is the Key to Success with online events. What we do when we join together is we spread business wide and cast a broader net. When we join with others the circle of influence grows, more contacts are made, and the more chance of leads, associates, or sales. I say advertising, you might catch one fish at a time if you're lucky but by networking and joining with others you are fishing with a net. It is spreading your business horizontally wide and far rather than vertically.

Networking is Vital online and not just being part of groups and posting ads. No one will take you serious if that is all you want to do. Rather it is about getting to know other people; people that

Save on Professional Fees, Plan Events Yourself

know other people and may become customers of yours once they get to know you. Volunteer, share, tips, articles, advice with others, and help our groups like this one or other Ryze or business communities, embrace live networking online and get to know the people behind the keyboards. Online events are cooperative Marketing and can be very vital. Imagine 20, 40, 60, or 100 business owners all joining together and reaping the benefits. These business owners work at a team so that everyone achieves more. The best use of online events, and there are many ways to make them successful, while sales are a general objective and certainly something to shoot for, you will find that once again you have to give people time to get to know you.

Collecting leads is another great goal for online parties, listing a newsletter or giveaways you can collect names and emails from but always ask for permission to contact people. Doing constant follow-ups is the key. Making new contacts is important; you will find common ground with others, and ways you can do joint ventures, for great ideas and finding ways to co-op your marketing. There is safety in numbers. Where you may spend hundreds of dollar offline for events most online events are under $20 many under $15 and some under $10. And if everyone is doing their part that can generate lots of traffic and leads in the two days to two weeks events are going on. But to make the most of it you must participate daily, not all day perhaps but drop in often, support others in events, make an effort, play a game, offer a prize, and get to know people.

Online events are one of the cheapest forms of marketing you can do, online or off and you can if not walk away with, as some might put it, TONS of sales (this rarely happens) walk away with Lots of contacts and some great well-earned education on how things happening online. If you are not a joiner, do not want to put forth an effort to be a part of a group, organizations or marketing cooperative then it is best that you do not even join as these groups depend on the efforts of all their members in the cooperatives. Unfortunately it means you are cheating not only yourself but other members if you are not willing to participate.

There are several styles of events to choose from; my advice is to find one that is supportive and offers you help and a group that is interactive and plugged in. You should feel you're a part of the group; not on your own.

3 Types of Online Events

- Free for all's, these are very busy fast paced events but also very confusing and disorganized. You find people trying to out-chat each other, vendors throwing out offers all day long, no real moderation unless someone that is not a vendor mistakenly put up a link then action is usually swift and unfriendly. Now no one that has not paid for an event should be promoting let's make that clear but I have seen some innocent people made to feel very unwelcome for making a mistake at such events. Moderators should Private message you if you make a mistake. And if you did not pay please do not attempt to promote your business at a sales event that is just not the proper way to network or get the word out.

- Time Slots, These events give you a set time, 30 minutes to an hour, and date(s) to show up and present your business events are generally a day to two or three days long. These generally have moderators who will keep things running smoothly for the group and welcome guests and may host games etc. They are effective and, if the vendors show up, run very smoothly. One drawback to such events is that often many vendors will only show up for their time slots and then leave right afterwards. Some do not spend time supporting the entire group and ignore other vendor's presentation. Most of the group will resent people that act this way, especially if it is an established group and one or two are seen as people that consistently do this. If you join any event you should support the event make time to spend there and be an active participant. It is up to the site owner and all vendors to get out and promote these events the more people participating the more advertising that should be seen. Often if you pay and miss your time there is no getting another chance, you lose that chance to present your business.

- Round Robin events: These work best for larger, more diverse groups, who have many members where it is hard to track who is going to be able to show up at which times. Some members may have jobs; some might have children and events or meetings to go to during the day or evening. What these events do is allow the group to come in as time allows and everyone gets a chance to present, generally in the order they arrived. Times can vary from 30 minutes with smaller group to 10 minutes with a larger group. Now ten minutes may seem short but we will get into presentation later on in this e-book and you will see that a well thought out and concise presentation can deliver a lot of information and keep people's attention even better than a longer 30 minute presentation does. It is all about delivering your presentation in a fun and effective manner.

Generally a list is made up to start and new people are added in as they come in. If someone is not paying attention when their time comes up they will get skipped. This is what is helpful at these day long events, there is a steady flow of people in and out all day long and they all know that they will have to wait a bit before getting to present their business and specials. Also, throughout the day, breaks are taken where all vendors are asked to post one special or their links so that everyone has more than one chance to share their links and those waiting can show a special before their turn comes up. It is up to the moderator to give everyone a chance and send messages if someone is going over their time or it is times up let's move on, however vendors are generally responsible to planning it out so they do not go over.

These events are easier for many people to attend as they do not have to fear losing out. You can drop in and plan on spending some time and getting a chance to present. Now one thing I don't recommend is waiting till the last hour, if you do that and many others do that also you might not get to present at all if time runs out.

Those are the three main types of events and you can try them all out or you can spend some time visiting and watching events to see which ones you might want to try out, what might fit your personal tastes. Look for a group that is friendly; that welcomes you as a guest. If they seem standoffish they probably are and those types of events might be hard to break into as a vendor. You want a group that is supportive of both members and guests and that welcomes questions.

Personally I do not stick around long if no one bothers to say hello to me at an event I am visiting. Guests want to be acknowledged much the same as you want a waiter or clerk in a store to say "hello" and "I will be right with you". Bottom line is, to reach success; you must find a group of people you feel comfortable with. If there is no group and not the support you feel you need; keep looking. You want to have the help getting started that you deserve and only a well-established well run site and group will do that for you. You want to find a leader that cares about you and the events and is there to offer advice or at least has a group set up that can offer you assistance getting started.

There are also sites that offer audio and video chatrooms not all are user friendly but might be for you. Our own group prefers the text chat and we use flashchat that is pretty much 98% user friendly as long as you have updates on Flash Player and a reliable connection. Dialup is acceptable however you might have to cut back on what is open to run almost any chatroom as they tend to take up a lot of resources on your computer. It is important to find a site that has chatrooms that work for you. It may however be your computer and you might have to consider upgrades. As things get faster online old, outdated computers will have issues. Also dial up vs. high speed access will also slow you down create lag, make it easier for you to be booted out of chatrooms.

It's Not Always about Sales

A misconception that many newbies have about events is that it has to be all about making sales. In reality while everyone want more sales the best use of the Media is getting the word out about your business, meeting people in a live format keyboard to keyboard, and building your business relationships and networking contacts.

Events are excellent opportunities to meet new people that share similar goals as you do to further their home-based businesses. It is an opportunity to share information, gather new contacts, and leads, find other that you can do some creative marketing with, and build relationships that will not only lead to sales if not right now, then down the road, and referrals as well. People to more business with people they know and trust. With scammers' rampant online and shady offers, live events are an excellent way to check out new businesses, and build trust with member and guest that are looking to do business with you. They are a good way to ask question about a business opportunity and get an answer about cost, quotas, and discounts right there.

Live events put you in front of real people who are there for two reasons, either like you to make new contacts and promote or guest who are looking for products or business opportunities. Now you need to find ways to collect leads, you can offer freebies they need to give you an email address for, play games, offer a newsletter, or simply say I would like to add you to my contact list, may I have you Instant messenger IDs or email address. It is important to ask at each and every show your ad. You goal should be not only to get sale but to add new contacts from each event you do. Have great deal if you want to get sales it is important to offer a sale exclusive to the event. A one-time offer they can get only if they buy now. This can be free shipping a super discount. But make the group understand that is it only for the Duration of that particular show that they will get your special deal. This should help increase your opportunity to get sales. Make sure you come away with at least some new contact at a show. Sometime it take a long time to get any sales do not give up. People again have to get to know you and trust you.

Don't be discouraged if you don't make a sale your first shows just try to get a few new contacts. And don't assume that online shows do not work because truly is it one of the most successful way to grow more business and one of the most affordable ways to grow more business online today. You just need to find your best deals and the right group of people to work with. And it takes time you should give a group or do at last 3 events before making up you mind if you wish to continue at that site or not. Your job is to make yourself someone people want to do business with and personable. You want to network and not just worry about making the sale up front. People do more business with people they get to know. Make sure they get to know you as someone worth doing business with. It is very important you show up and support the show

Save on Professional Fees, Plan Events Yourself
entirely not just show up and do your presentation and leave. You
need to support the group to build trust.

Chapter 8- Planning an Event on a Fixed Budget

Your event suppliers are everything to a party. You need to have the best, never second best. However, you need to keep good relationships with event supplies or they will never work for you ever. You can be ruined in a matter of minutes when you do something to hurt your relationship with a supplier.

One of the most important reasons why you need to be nice when dealing with your supplies is because they make or break you. If you disrespect the supplier, they will not only work for you, but they will tell everyone about you. You will end up losing your business or reputation based on the fact that you weren't worth working for.

Again, your suppliers can make and break you, if you mess with the best; you then have to look at second-rate suppliers. Not only will your guests notice the change, but also they aren't as worth the money. You may find that they show up late or they don't deliver quality, and then your friends and associates are looking at your like what happened. You will lose cliental, you will lose friends, and you will lose associates because who wants to go to a party that is way below the normal standard?

The next reason why you should be nice to your even suppliers is because your guests will come accustom to a certain standard. If you lose your suppliers, your guests will notice. If you aren't finding better suppliers to replace the older ones, you may end up losing your good reputation and have a fall from grace. You will notice that people will begin talking about you and you will feel ruined and be on the defense every time. Your supplies not only make the party, but they have a direct effect on your reputation and pull.

The fourth reason to be nice to your suppliers is because they sometimes will offer you things that you wouldn't normally get from them. If you have a strong relationship with your suppliers they will begin to give you better quality of things and offer you great discounts. You will be able to relay on them for anything. With that said, comes the fifth reason.

The fifth reason is tied with the benefits of having a strong and solid relationship. Basically, you can begin to lean on them. You can begin to plan a party within a week or two and they are willing to cancel any other contract to please you. If they overbook, they are more likely to choose you over the other. You begin to have a loyal relationship with them and they are more willing to go out of their way for you.

The next reason is based on their loyalty and trust for you. They may end up giving you or your clients' extensions to pay the balance off. They will open a credit account with you so that you don't have to worry about quickly transferring the money. They will, in fact, give you a payment plan that they only offer to those who they have had long term connections with.

The seventh reason why you need to play nice with the supplies is the fact that they can back out at any time and then you are stuck to find another supplier for the event or party. It can be such a hassle to replace last minute quitters. It's also very expensive.

The eight reasons to be nice is all the money that you can save. You will get discounts, extras, lower fees, and everything that concerns money once you have showed that you are worth the benefit. If they like you personally, you are more likely to save some money or get a kick back for the event.

How and Where to Find the Best Suppliers

It's hard to find a supplier that will move mountains for you, but you need to look at it in two different lights. If you are nice to your suppliers and you are able to build a trusting relationship, both of you can benefit. There is a reason for a supplier to go the extra mile for your event and it comes in the form of good reputations and recommendations. However, you need to build a trusting relationship by using the one supplier each time. After use, they will know you better and care for you. Regulars always get the special treatment, but you have to build the trust the get that type of supplier.

You should know that your supplier wants to build relationships with its clients. This is important because you are already half way to building a trusting and strong tie. The other part depends on you. You have to explain what you want, but go about it in a good way. Don't call them upset because something didn't work out. That is when you talk in a low and calm voice and ask what can be done.

Save on Professional Fees, Plan Events Yourself

To get a supplier that will move mountains for you, you have to realize the difference between being nice and kissing up. You don't need to kiss up, but you need to be respectful and show some curtsey. You can say things that are negative without saying it in a negative way. Meaning, you can state that your upset, but not to the point where it offends someone. The trick to not offending anyone is to personalize compliments and then de-personalize negative compliments. This way no one will offend by anything that you say.

Now, there are a lot of suppliers who think the world of themselves and tend to be easily offended and disrespectful. These suppliers are harder to build a relationship with. They aren't willing to build a relationship or go the extra mile for anyone. This is when you look for another supplier who is willing to work with you. How do you do this? Well, begin to ask around. Ask your friends, co-workers, and family whom you should hire to do the work. This way you can make a business relationship with a supplier who is friendly and willing to help you with your event or party. They may not want to move mountains for you, but they will want to work with you.

Once you find a supplier who wants to work with you, you will want to state the type of business relationship that you are looking for. You should talk to the supplier and tell them that you are looking for someone who will be loyal and help them deliver a great party. You will want to tell them that they will get all your business if they do a good job with you. You may even want to sign a contract stating that you will only work with them until the other party has shown clear signs of disrespect and low quality. This is what will help form a lasting business relationship. Once you have a long lasting business relationship, you will find that they are willing to do whatever it takes to make you happy.

Linda Smith

There is a lot of work to do with building business relationships with other businesses. You need to be willing to make a lasting impression and be respectful to the supply. They too need to be willing, loyal, and respectful for the relationship to work to your advantage. You need to make sure that you put a lot of time and effort into the relationship or it will not work.

Choosing the Right Suppliers

You have to be careful when you are trying to plan a great event. You need to make sure that you are using the right vendors that are there to help you. There are many different people out there that want to take your money and you need to make sure that you are protecting yourself and your event when you decide to use them.

Planning the perfect event for any reason is something that anyone wants to do. It is not always easy; however it is something that you have to take seriously because you will want to make sure that you are getting the most for your money. You want to get the most for your money, but yet still put on a great event.

Shop around for prices on what you need. For example, if you need fifty table clothes, don't get them at the first store that you come to, call at least three suppliers and ask their prices on that same item. That item could be just $1 cheaper at another store, and shipped free, compared to paying $1 more for each table cloth and to have to pay shipping as well.

Look for items that you can reuse at other events. For example, go back to the back to the table cloth order. Will you be able to launder the items, cheap, and reuse them again at another event? This is a good idea is you are going to be an event planner or put on a lot of different events in the next few months or years. While it could be a little more costly up front instead of using paper, you have to look at the number of times you can use these table clothes, and the price you would pay each time if you were to use paper. Remember, savvy affairs and events are not the place for paper anyway, so you might end up buying paper table clothes for four events, and then still have to purchase those linens for another event.

A supplier can make or break your event, just by not showing up. You need to keep a list of supplies that are local so that just in case you find your supplier does not ship or doesn't show, you can purchase what you need, without waiting. You always need a backup plan. For example, the 125 paper table clothes you orders online that are blue and green, can you get them anywhere else locally, within fifty miles, even if it costs more? If your supplier doesn't show, or doesn't ship and it is the day of the event, you need to send someone to your backup, and get what you need. Don't let anyone hold you up from being successful.

Hold people to their contracts, to what you ordered. If you ordered 100 green cloth napkins and 40 black napkins for centerpieces, and your shipped the products but in backwards amounts, call the supplier. Tell them you want a big discount or you are going to refuse to accept the shipment. Make your point known. If you have to put up with items that are wrong, then get a discount; get money back on the overall deal. Make it or break it, which is all a name of the game. You can be strong with vendors, remember you are paying their bill and you don't have to pay for what is right. Make the vendor or supplier work for your money.

You should avoid vendors and suppliers who are always running late. Avoid suppliers that do not deliver what you order, and in the quantities that you always order. Keep a running list of suppliers that will put you on top of everything from forks, to tables, to food, to lighting and candles. Always know where you bought the item last and at least one other supplier for that item so your events will 'go off' without a hitch.

Organizing an Event with a Small Budget

When you want to have a great event, but you have to do it on a budget, you will want to make sure that you are finding ways to cut your expenses. There are many different things that you will have to pay for and you will want to make sure that you are able to get all that you need with the money that you have set for the party.

The first thing that you will need to do is figure out what your budget is and what you need to do to stay on it. There are many ways that you can stray away from your budget and you will want to make sure that you stay on track and keep your budget in play. Here are a few ideas when creating an event on a shoestring budget.

1. You will first want to find ways to save money. This is most important. However you do not want to go too cheap if you do not have to. You want to stay on the proposed budget and not take shortcuts that you do not have to.

2. The next way to save money is to find all the friends and family members that you can to help you out with your party. You do not want to have to hire people unless you have to. If you can save money by having volunteers help, you should take advantage of it.

3. Shop wisely. You will want to try and bargain shop any time that you can. This will help you save money so that you can get the materials that you will need and not have to spend your entire budget on the things that you need. You will also want to shop as

much as you can so that you can find the discounts that will help you with your shoestring budget.

4. Donations are a great way to save money. If you know someone that can help you with your party, you should ask them for a contribution. This will help you raise money that you find necessary to get the things done that you need. You will find that a lot of people like to help out for a good cause.

5. You need to find a location that will be very inexpensive. You want to get a location that will make your party great but also save you money in the long run. You will want to make sure that you are first finding out if the location that you have is going to be the better place for the event. You will want to shop around until you find the price that fits your budget as well as accommodates all your needs.

Make the food for your event. You need to have food and appetizers for your event. You will find that you can save a lot of money for your budget when you decide to make the food. Buying or hiring someone to make everything for your event can sometimes become expensive. You will want to make sure that you are allowing enough in your budget to get all the food that you need to make your event a great success.

6. Advertising can take up a big part of your budget. You will want to try and get your event out there for the public to know about. However you will not want to over spend on your budget for this. You want to try and find inexpensive ways to get your event advertised. You can use the local newspapers or make up your own flyers to hand out.

7. There is nothing wrong with trying to make a deal with the things that you need. You will want to try and get the cheaper price for

just about anything that you are going to need. This will be a good way for you to save money and get the better deal that will fit your shoestring budget.

Ask for support from your community. You will want to try and find the support that you need to make your event happen. You can ask anyone that you know to help out as much as they can. This will give you a break and let you relax a little more when it comes time for the event to happen

About The Author

Linda Smith is a mother and certified thrift police. Unwilling to spend even a single penny for professional services, Linda took the time to learn every job so she can mimic and perform.

Linda grew up in a farm in Tennessee. She was the fourth child in a family of twelve. Life in her early years wasn't easy. They had to share what little food there is and often went to school with only an apple for lunch. Her tough and underprivileged childhood molded Linda to who she is today — a resilient and extremely resourceful woman.